THE FATE OF A CONTINENT

THE FATE OF A CONTINENT

JIMMY ANYWAR

Published by Sahel Publishing Association
P.O. Box 18007—00100
Nairobi, Kenya
Tel: +011-254-715-596-106
www.sahelpublishing.net

A Sahel Book
Editor: Sam Okello
Interior design: Hellen Wahonya Okello
Cover design: Peter Omamo
Images: Jimmy Anywar
Author contact: janywar@hotmail.com

–
Printed in India, U.K., and U.S.A.

My mother, Lamunu
My late father, Sekondo Ojok
My children, Elisabeth, Robert, and Anthony

TABLE OF CONTENTS

TABLE OF CONTENTS

INTRODUCTION

I am an African born in Acholi, Northern Uganda. My father, Sekondo Ojok, was a Medical Assistant and my mother, Lamunu, is a housewife. I was raised and educated in Gulu. I attended Lacor Primary School, St. Joseph's Junior Secondary School, and St. Joseph's College Layibi. I then joined Uganda College of Commerce, Nakawa, but left without completing the course to join Bank of Uganda. This was of course a mistake. I joined Bank of Uganda as a clerk in the Accounts Department. Here I was lucky because within a short time I got a scholarship to train in banking in the Federal Republic of Germany. The course terminated with a diploma. I then returned to Uganda and continued to work for Bank of Uganda.

Within weeks of my return to Uganda, the country faced a tragedy. A military coup took place and brought General Idi Amin to power. This will go down in Uganda's history as the worst time the country ever went through. The rule of law broke down and a lot of killings of innocent citizens took place. The coup took place in January 1971. Idi Amin was a general in the Ugandan Army at that time (see picture next page). He overthrew the government of Milton Obote, who had ruled Uganda since independence in 1962. Obote's government was unpopular among the Baganda, so Idi Amin's coup found great support among them. I was in Kampala the day the coup took place. Some gunshots were heard during the night and in the morning radio announcements were made asking people to stay at home and that Obote's government had been overthrown. The coup itself was bloodless because there was no resistance. There was a huge celebration in and around Kampala.

General Idi Amin; became President of Uganda through a military coup on 25ᵗʰ January, 1971. He was driven out of power by a military invasion led by Tanzanian troops and Ugandan exiles in 1979.

As usual, the military promised to hand over power to a democratically elected government in the shortest possible time. A government of national unity was formed and reputable technocrats were appointed ministers. Meanwhile, Amin started consolidating his power by eliminating potential opponents. The Acholis, one of the many tribal groups in Uganda, were particularly targeted. They were the biggest single tribe in the army and the police. Before independence, the British authority recruited many Acholis in the military and the police because they were tall and well built men who were also very loyal. The other tribes did not like to join the military because they said it was only for the uneducated. The Acholis in the military were Idi Amin's first target. Massive killings of Acholis and Langis were carried out in military barracks.

After cleansing the military and the police of the Acholis and Langis, Amin's men turned on the civilian Acholi and Lango population. The Acholis and Langis were picked from their homes and offices never to be seen again. I was an Assistant Currency Officer at Jinja Currency Centre. Jinja town is situated about eighty kilometres northeast of the capital, Kampala. One evening I went out to the Police Mess (club for Police Officers) to meet some friends and have a game of darts. As soon as I entered the club, my friends who were Police Officers came to me and advised me to leave immediately because some Army Officers were there looking for me earlier on. I obliged and left and thanked them for the information, which saved my life. When I told my boss in Kampala the next morning that the military was looking for me, he advised me to leave Jinja town immediately and return to Kampala. I handed over the vault keys to the secretary, went to the Hotel and checked out and left for Kampala. I started planning to leave the Country, because it was only a matter of time before they would find out my whereabouts. Many of my tribesmen were being picked up from their homes and offices, tortured and murdered in cold blood. As Amin and his henchmen continued killing the Acholis and the Langis, there was no word of condemnation from the other tribes. However, it was not long before Amins barbarism became apparent to all Ugandans. He expelled all Asians out of Uganda and made it extremely difficult for ordinary Ugandans to leave the country. Through good contacts, I managed to obtain a ticket to fly out to Frankfurt am Main. Idi Amin began killing people indiscriminately and those technocrats in his government started fleeing the country. The mistake he made, which probably caused his isolation and rapid downfall, was the killing of the Archbishop of Church of Uganda, Janani Luwum, RIP; the killing of the Chief Justice and former Prime Minister, Benedicto Kiwanuka, RIP; and the killing of two of his own cabinet ministers, Erinayo Wilson Oryema, RIP, and Charles Oboth Ofumbi, RIP.

I have lived in Germany ever since and have now become a German citizen. At this point, I would like to thank the German authorities for offering me asylum at that very difficult time. I hope that those of you, young ones, will not find it necessary to have to flee your countries to save your lives.

One of the reasons I have decided to write this book is to encourage Africa's youth to be more active and involved in the shaping of affairs in your respective countries and in the continent as a whole. It is a shame that even today, five decades after independence, many young Africans die trying to reach Europe. Some of them get drowned and some are killed on the way, for their organs (heart, lungs, kidneys, etc.). These young Africans are not leaving their countries voluntarily, but because they do not see any future in their own countries of birth. African leaders have let down their own people. There is widespread corruption and nepotism. The most unfortunate thing is that even if governments change nothing really changes, corruption and bad governance continue unabated. This is why I am appealing to today's youth to help bring about change. The future is yours and it is up to you to fight for a better future. Africa is very rich with minerals and commodities and with proper planning and management, you can, indeed make it a flourishing continent. Fleeing your country is not the answer. Remember that those countries that are today well developed attained this over many years through hard work and good governance. You all have dreams, may be of becoming medical doctors, owning houses, cars, and so on. This can only be possible if you start working for change now.

CHAPTER ONE

Education

I am hoping that this book will be out in the year 2013, when I will have reached the age of 65. I actually never thought I would become so old; that is why I am so pleased to be able to share with you some of my life experiences and give you some advice that can make your life better. At 65 I am slowly reaching the end of my biological life. Looking back, I realize would have done many things differently with the experiences I went through. You should consider yourself lucky to read this book because some of the advices here will genuinely help you make the right decisions in the course of your life.

Life is something like a journey. The journey begins with your birth and ends with old age. It is a long journey with many obstacles. You have to be brave and fearless to make it through to the end (old age). Remember, irrespective of your colour: black, brown, white or yellow, you are all born equal. It is after birth that things begin to take different directions. Those of you from wealthy parents will have advantages over those from poor parents because you will have easier access to facilities like better schools, books, computers and the internet, television, and so on. All the same education is a must for all.

If life is like a journey, education is the passport for this journey. When you successfully complete your education you will be awarded a certificate, a diploma, or a degree. This is a one-time achievement and nobody can take it away from you.

Since education is a must, every child, boy or girl, must be given a chance to attend school. Basic education must be free for all. Higher education must be facilitated. By this I mean that if you want to join a university but you do not have a scholarship or anybody to pay the fees, you should be given a chance to take a loan that is repayable after completion. There are many, young bright Africans out there who have failed to continue with their education because of failure to pay fees.

African governments should put education at the top of all priorities. Recently, in a Ugandan newspaper, the *Daily Monitor*, I saw a picture of children learning under a tree instead of in a classroom. Unfortunately this kind of scene is not only in Uganda, but in many African countries. African governments can afford to spend billions of dollars on military equipment like fighter jets, helicopters, tanks, and so on and leave school children to learn under trees or in classrooms without a roof. African governments can afford to buy luxury vehicles for its officials, like Mercedes Benzes, BMWs, 4 Wheel drives, and so on and leave children to go schooling hungry for the whole day. I was in fact shocked in February 2013 to read a newspaper article that a school in north-western Uganda provided lessons to its pupils under trees for over twenty years. The school was started by parents who were tired of watching their children walk for about ten kilometres every day to the nearest school. It was taken over by the government in 2000. These parents were only able to construct a building with two rooms which were used by the first and seventh classes and the rest of the classes were being conducted under trees. Those learning under trees had no desks and they sat on logs of wood and stones and they had to flee every time it rained. This is unacceptable, and yet within the last twenty years or so, the government was able to purchase thousands of luxury vehicles, residential jets, military helicopters, and so on. I can go on listing things that are not right today but it will not change anything. You are the ones who will be in leadership positions in years to come and you should address these injustices yourselves.

Let me propose one thing that can wipe out illiteracy in Africa. In 5 decades of independence, African countries have received billions of dollars in foreign aid. Today, many African countries still receive aid and budget support. Most of this aid is often mismanaged or stolen and donor countries will agree with me here.

My proposal is that aid and budget support should stop altogether. Instead, donor countries should encourage interested African countries to set up an independent African Education Authority (AEA), directly and financially answerable to the donor countries. All aid money will be channelled directly to the AEA purely for educational purposes. Each government will be responsible for the syllabuses, curriculum and examinations, but this can be harmonised to be the same throughout Africa. The governments can still borrow money for infrastructural development and so on, but the loan has to be repaid and may be this will bring some sense as to how and on what governments can spend money on.

Almost in all African countries, schools and colleges, except the new ones, are in very bad shape and totally underequipped. Teachers have no houses and often have to travel long distances to get to school or college and are often late or absent and on top of that, they are badly paid (underpaid). In fact in Uganda today primary school teachers are paid a monthly salary that is the equivalent of a weekly allowance of a member of parliament.

Many schools and colleges have no sports facilities, no laboratory, and no library. Sport is indeed vital in a place of learning because it keeps you fit and healthy and your mind is left free to concentrate and absorb the stuff you are learning. Africa could provide the world with top sportsmen and sportswomen if only the youth could be given the opportunity to start early with the kind of sports they are interested in. Today, all schools and colleges should, in addition to athletics, provide facilities for football, basketball, volleyball, handball, tennis and table tennis. The earlier you start playing these games the better you become, and for the very talented players, may be they can become international professional players.

At this early stage when you start playing games you will be competing with other players and teams from within or outside your school or college. Something very important you must learn at this very early stage is Sportsmanship and Fair Play. Remember, in a competition you would like to win, but also does your opponent. Both sides should stick to sportsmanship and fair play to attain this goal. It hurts a lot the moment you lose a game, but remember that this is only a game and there will still be many more games in the future and if you prepare yourself better next time you will also win.

A good example here is the 2011/2012 European Champions League football final. Bayern Munich did everything to reach the final, which was to be played in their stadium. With the home advantage in their favour, they thought they would easily win. As it happened, Chelsea put up a strong fight, and after extra time, there match was a draw. There was penalty shooting to decide the winner, and Chelsea had more luck and won. Loosing in their stadium was especially painful for Bayern Munich, but they had to accept it and live with it. This year, 2012/2013 season, they are again in the final against Borussia Dortmund. The final will be played in Wembley Stadium, and I think this time they are better prepared to win. Fans too have to learn to be fair irrespective of the rivalries between the teams. It is unfortunate that even today in Europe some fans are still violent and even racial. A game should actually be looked at as an entertainment for all spectators and if your team wins, well and fine, rejoice it, but if your team loses take it easy and hope that they will win next time. Violence and insults will not change the result.

Indeed education begins at home. It is at home that you begin to learn good manners, respect, and other values which will guide you throughout your life. This early home education is very important because it is going to shape your character. Parents should remember that they are their children's heroes. Children admire their parents and would like to be like them when they become older. Laws should be passed requiring parents to register all births and made responsible for the child's education from the beginning. Failure to send a child to school should be punishable by a fine.

Education is very important and it will play a major role in every child's future. That is why education should be free from the beginning till university entry so that every child has a chance. A bright child should not be denied university education because of lack of money to pay fees. In many developed countries there are financial programmes to help such students to continue with their higher education. These programmes allow a student to borrow money at low interest for the duration of the studies, and the money is repayable in small instalments when the student completes his studies and gets a job. In some countries a student is required to pay back only half of this loan and in some countries a student gets exempted at the end. This kind of programme gives a fair and equal opportunity to all. The best time to study is now when you are still young and you should use this opportunity to go for the highest and best qualifications possible. Whatever qualifications you attain, it is an achievement that will escort you throughout your life and no one will ever take it away from you.

Education opens the world's door for you. You can become a medical doctor, a lawyer, an engineer, an architect, an accountant, a pilot, and so on if you take your studies seriously and excel. If you have a chance to learn foreign languages do not hesitate to learn them. The world has become global and any foreign language you learn will be a great asset in your future. African governments must also encourage students to specialise in medical and other science subjects. In some countries with a population of over 20 million, there are less than 100 qualified Opticians, less than 100 qualified Chemists, just to mention two professions. This leaves a lot to be desired.

By now you should be pretty clear about what you want to be or do in the future. When you complete your studies, you will enter another phase of life, that of a career. Jobs will be hard to find but with a well educated population, investors will find it attractive and will come and invest, thereby providing good job opportunities. You will have made many friends and acquaintances all these years. Be careful with whom you socialise. There are cliques out there consuming drugs and alcohol. They will tell you how "nice" it is to feel "high". They will tell you that you will forget all your problems after consumption. Yes, you may forget all your problems, but when the drug effects are over, the problems will still be there.

When you are young, you are very energetic and inquisitive. You will hear talk about alcohol, drugs, cigarettes, and gambling. Due to human curiosity, you might want to try these out yourself. My father used to smoke a pipe, but forbade us (all his children) from smoking. His argument was that smoking cigarettes was unhealthy and expensive. He was right when I now look back. My father was humble and never picked up any quarrel with his neighbours. He was a Catholic. He studied in a seminary school and nearly became a priest. After he decided not to become a priest, he trained as a medical assistant. He worked in Kitgum Hospital and at Lacekocot Hospital in East Acholi before he retired in 1961.

He later developed Alzheimer's disease and died. I always followed his advices and never attempted to smoke until I started to work. At work, during coffee breaks, I could see colleagues drinking coffee and smoking, thereby gently blowing out smoke. I was very attracted to this and decided to try it myself. Fortunately for me, I always developed a headache in the afternoon whenever I smoked. So after three days, the curiosity was over. Since that day, I have not been a smoker. Some years later in a pub in Germany, an acquaintance offered me a joint to try (tobacco mixed with hash). I tried it but did not find anything nice about it and neither was there any aftereffect on me so I never got involved with it again. Alcohol consumption was also forbidden for the young ones. The first time I drank alcohol was when I was seventeen years old. It was during the holidays when two of my school mates, Christopher Owor and Anthony Aluku, came to visit me. They were some years older than me so they wanted to drink something alcoholic. I asked my stepsister Dorin if she could get us some local brew. Luckily, her mother had prepared some and she had gone to the forest to collect some firewood. To be honest, the brew was a bit sweet and tasted very nice. Dorin was very generous and gave us plenty to drink for free. The result was that we all felt "high" and adventurous.

Due to alcohol, we became very bold and decided to go for a flirt in a nearby girl's boarding school (Sacred Heart Senior Secondary). It was illegal to enter the school compound that day because visitors were not allowed. To make a long story short, I spent the night in police custody, charged with trespassing. However, since I did not commit any other offence and I was a minor, I was released the next day. I learnt a lot about alcohol this one time. Alcohol negatively changes your personality and behaviour and makes you aggressive and insolent. Regular and excess consumption of alcohol is very dangerous. You can become addicted to it and it can badly ruin your health. Gambling is also a bad habit. It usually starts harmlessly. Imagine you go to a pub and you slot a coin in a slot machine and all of a sudden you win fifty dollars. From now on you will always slot coins in the machine whenever you find one. If you get addicted to playing these machines, you will end up bankrupt because these machines are programmed in such a way that your chance of winning is less than five percent. Remember that any game you play, there is always an element of luck. This element of luck varies from day to day and time to time. There are days when your luck is good and you win, but there are also days when your luck is bad and you lose. I have seen people spending hundreds of dollars playing lotto whenever the jackpot was high. Something that they forget about is the luck factor. They can spend thousands of dollars playing lotto but if luck is not on their side, they will lose. On the other hand, somebody lucky can play just for one dollar and win the jackpot. My advice to you is:

1) Completely avoid smoking;
2) Do not consume any drugs;
3) avoid heavy alcohol consumption;
4) avoid all gambling.

If you follow my advice, you will live a very good life.

CHAPTER TWO

Religion

Religion is a particular system of faith and worship that relates humanity to spirituality and moral values. Parents normally want their children to belong to the same faith as they. They send their children to schools that teach their faith. There are many religions in Africa, but only three main ones: Catholic, Protestant, and Muslim. In school, you start to learn early the values of humanity and spirituality. Through religion, you learn that there is a God who helps you go through your daily life. Although each religion teaches you about a deity, I personally believe that this is the same and the only one God that exists. I believe that there is some supernatural power and this is God. Since there is only one God for all human beings, it would be total nonsense to tell anybody that my God or my religion is better than the others. Every day we pray to the same God. It is the way we worship God that differs from one religion or church to another.

I was raised a Catholic and I attended only Catholic schools throughout my education. I had Protestant neighbours who also sent their children to Protestant schools. There was also a Muslim neighbour who sent his children to either a Catholic or Protestant school because there was no Muslim school nearby. I personally got along very well with all my neighbours and their children. I was an active Catholic and was at one time President of the Young Christian Society.

When you are young you are not very critical and you tend to unquestionably accept all the teachings of your religion or church. But as you grow older you also become more critical. As a young man I accepted all the teachings of the church, yet today I do not agree with all the teachings or views of the church. As you grow older you can freely choose your system of worship, in other words you can change your religion as you choose. However, this must be a totally free choice. You have to learn to accept and respect other religions.

There are individuals out there who are only bent on creating hatred among different religious believers. Recently I read a newspaper report of the closure of an illegal school in Uganda. There were supposedly over thirty children in this school and they were only being taught one subject. The subject was Arabic, with emphasis on the Quran. When the children were asked why they were not being taught other subjects like English, or Arithmetic, or Geography, which was taught in other schools, they replied that the Sheikh, who was the owner of the school, told them that the other subjects were satanic and that the Quran forbids them. This is grotesque! If it was true, there would be no Muslim doctors or engineers because before they qualified they had to learn these subjects, right? This is how people, like this Sheikh, manipulate children in Uganda, Africa and other parts of the world. These are the kind of people who will tell children to commit horrific crimes and if they die in the process, they will go to paradise where milk and honey is in abundance.

Let me assure you here that there is no such place called paradise. Paradise is only the imagination of a place where all human beings want to go when they die. Nobody has been there to come back and tell us that there is such a place and what it is like.

Religious tolerance is important if this world is to live in peace and harmony. Nobody should be forced to join a religion or a church. In some African countries you still hear of people being slaughtered for belonging to a religion, why? This is deplorable. These slaughtered people were human beings just like their killers, but they believed in their way of worshipping God—the same God that their killers also worshipped. Belonging to a certain religion or church does not make you a Satan or an Angel. Whether you are a Muslim or a Protestant or a Catholic, you are all human beings with equal rights. You should be left alone to worship God the way you find fit. A good religion or church does not use force to convert believers. Also belonging to a certain religion that is a majority in that country does not make you a superior citizen to the other citizens of minority religions. Religion should not create hatred but peace, love, and harmony among people.

All religions teach us to love one another. No religion advocates killing as a means of a solution. Killing is unforgivable and God will punish those who kill. Suicide bombers will always end up in hell. There is no cause whatsoever for anybody to massively kill innocent people.

God gave us the gift of life and it is only Him that can take it away.

In the course of your life, you will hear a lot about myths, rituals and cults. Any religion, church, or organisation that performs rituals where human beings are sacrificed should have no place in our society. God does not want any sacrifice from us. In times of trouble, when you have many problems, pray to God for help and be patient; God will help you. Many people in Africa turn to witchcraft in times of trouble. This is wrong. First of all the witchdoctor is not going to help you for nothing. Secondly, there is no guarantee of success. Thirdly, the solution might require the sacrifice of an innocent life. I was shocked to read a story of a young man in Kampala who doused his wife with chloroform and abducted his two month old son in the dead of the night.

Two days later the remains of the child was found in a nearby bush by residents living nearby. Allegedly the child's tongue had been ripped out and private parts severed off. The man of course denied killing the child, but on further questioning he confessed that he had taken the child to a witchdoctor for ritual sacrifice so that he could amass wealth. This is a chilling story and unfortunately this kind of crime is happening every day somewhere in Africa. This young man has ruined his life. He is not going to amass any wealth and has deprived his son of a God-given right to live; and he may spend the rest of his life in prison. These kinds of people must be imprisoned for life and, to avoid more senseless loss of life, they must be forced to identify the witchdoctors so that they are weeded out.

Let me appeal to you not to believe in witchcraft. Wealth, success, and good health can only be attained by your own efforts with the help of God. Do not believe anybody who prophesises riches if you do a certain ritual. The way to riches is through hard work. Billionaires like Bill Gates and Warren Buffett did not have to go through rituals to get rich; they worked hard and were innovative and successful.

If you are sick and somebody tells you to perform a ritual in order to be healed, do not believe it. No ritual on earth will cure a sickness. The only way of healing is to understand your sickness better by consulting medical doctors and probably making adjustments in your lifestyle. Leave witchcraft and superstition alone. Witchdoctors are dubious business people who are only out to make money from you. They say they can help you if you fulfil a condition and pay them a fee, but do they really? If you fulfil the condition and pay the fee, he probably performs a ritual. After the ritual nothing happens because it is bogus, but he will have taken your money. You cannot take him to the police because you yourself might have committed a capital offence, (killing somebody to obtain the organs for the ritual), and even if you are not found out, you will live with a guilty conscience for the rest of your life.

Before I move on to the next chapter, let me tell you another interesting story about an alleged power of witchcraft. In the 1980s in Uganda, a young woman called Lakwena formed a church called the Holy Spirit Movement. This movement vowed to fight and overthrow the then government with their bare hands and the power of witchcraft. The believers, who were also the fighters, were told to smear oil on their skins. This oil would protect them against bullets because bullets would bounce off. They were also told that they did not need any guns; all they had to carry were stones which allegedly would turn into grenades when thrown at government troops. Many people also believed that Lakwena herself would instantly turn into a monkey whenever government soldiers closed in on her. One of her followers was surprisingly a University Professor. The Holy Spirit Movement was wiped out in one day of encounter with government forces and Lakwena escaped to Kenya where she eventually died in exile.

CHAPTER THREE

Career

You will probably start work with a private company or with a government department if you are lucky. I am saying lucky because youth unemployment rate is very high in African countries and on top of that you may be confronted with ethnic or tribal problems. In many countries in Africa the government is the biggest employer, and if you happen not to come from the ruling tribe or ethnic group, you are likely not to get a government job irrespective of your high qualifications. Governments are not doing enough to create jobs, yet they cannot rely on investors to create jobs for them. They have to create government corporations that can offer employment to fresh graduates every year. These corporations may not make huge profits nor make losses, but offer employment. With time and good development, the government can sell off these corporations. This is the way it worked in many developed countries. In fact Germany owned and kept control of the railways, telecommunications and postal businesses up to the end of the twentieth century. Today the government is still partly in control of Volkswagen.

African governments should be more innovative. They can, for instance, set up research centres for tropical medicine, for renewable energy, for agricultural products and so on. Research is normally a long-term project and this could help in the intake of university leavers every year. With time and some success, international companies and organisations will become interested and help fund part or whole of the research programmes. With research, Africa will be able to find solutions to problems we have not been able to solve without help. If I may mention one problem which has been there since my childhood, it is malaria! This disease is still widespread in Africa. Every minute, malaria is killing somebody in Africa. Why don't African countries come together and set up a malaria research centre, whose aim is to eradicate the disease? The problem is that African governments cannot or do not want to take the initiative to solve a problem. The attitude is that the Europeans or the Americans will solve it. This attitude is wrong and you young ones have got to change it. Face all challenges boldly and resolutely. Nothing is impossible!

Many African governments send their officials for medical treatment abroad, thereby incurring costs of about 200 million US dollars every year. Can you imagine what this money could do every year? The government could build a new hospital every year and fully equip it with all kinds of modern gadgets. In many African countries people still have to travel up to 100 kilometres or more to reach a hospital for treatment. If the government stops or drastically reduces the number of those officials treated abroad, the money saved could be used to build a new hospital every year. The first year build one in the centre of the country, the next year in the north of the country, then in the east, then in the west and so on as the need arises. Within 20 years hospital infrastructure and medical services will have reached dynamic levels.

When you are looking for a job, have a very clear vision of what you want to do in life. A successful career depends on the goals you want to achieve, short-term, mid-term, and long-term. Make the most of the resources and opportunities you come through. Whatever job you are doing, the skills and experience you are gaining are important for your future development. Be on the look out for opportunities to improve your qualifications. As you polish your skills and consolidate your experience, keep your eyes open for opportunities for upward mobility. If you are a medical doctor, a lawyer, or an architect, take a venture and set up your own practice. It will not be easy, but with hard work, courage, fortitude, steadfastness and tenacity you will succeed. Competition will be hard, but if you strive for excellence in whatever you do, you will always end up on top.

If you decide to change your job, money alone should not be the main factor. There are other important factors like job security and opportunities for exposure and experience. Some years back, a friend of mine who was working in a well established company as an engineer saw a newspaper advertisement for the same kind of job with another company. The other company was offering more money so he applied for the job and got it. Within one year, the new company became bankrupt and he lost his job. He remained unemployed for many months and deeply regretted his action.

Be a team player and be respectful of your fellow colleagues. Reliability, honesty, and punctuality should be the cornerstone virtues of your career. It is also important to start to learn to live within your means. By this I mean that if you earn 500 dollars net a month, you should try not to spend a dollar more than this amount in a month. Let us assume that you really need to spend 501 dollars every month, your account will be minus one dollar at the beginning of the second month. When your salary comes in at the end of the second month, you will only have 499 dollars in your account and if you require 501 you will have to overdraw your account by 2 dollars. By the end of the year your account will have been overdrawn by well over 60 dollars, plus interest. I am only trying to demonstrate how fast you can get into debt even if you start with minimal amounts; and you must remember that the overdraft has to be repaid at some stage.

When I was young, I was never taught how to use my money and I never budgeted. This was wrong because I used my money carelessly and very often I overdrew my bank account. Let me appeal to you to heed my advice. Live within your means and you will not regret it. If you can save some money every month please do so. Life has got its ups and downs and if you happen to hit the downs you will be happy that you happened to have saved some money. My son Robert once told me a story which made me very proud of him. He told me that he was one time involved in a motor accident; somebody hit him at the back but fortunately nobody was hurt. Since he was not at fault, the insurance of the other vehicle offered to pay him for the value of the car as it was, because it was economically illogical to repair it. He accepted the offer. He was paid a lump sum and he used only 25% of the money to repair it in a local garage. Then I asked him what he did with the rest of the money. "I put it in the Bank for bad times ahead," he said. This made me very proud of him because he proved to me that he was financially responsible.

As you go along, you are growing older and probably earning more. You will begin to acquire some domestic equipment like radio, computer, television, refrigerator, and so on. These are standard things for home comfort and they are usually not very expensive. Be careful if you decide to buy a car. It is very easy to raise the amount for buying a car. What many people do not consider before purchasing a vehicle are the running and maintenance costs. Before you buy a car, new or second hand, calculate what it will cost you to drive it to work and back. Can you afford to pay for spare parts and repair costs should something go wrong? If you are able to meet all the costs without financial trouble then go ahead and buy it. But even then I would advise you to start with a small car with low consumption.

The best investment at a young age is purchasing a flat or a house. Unfortunately I did not make this investment in my young days although I had the opportunity. My excuse was that buying a property in a certain place would for ever tie me down to that place. Looking back today, it was a mistake because I could have sold the property if I were to move to another place or town. Whatever property you decide to buy, do not overburden yourself with debt. Any investment you make should be with a focus to the future. Ask yourself whether you want to marry and have children. And if you can start a small business so much the better.

Most young Africans tend to be lazy and this has to change in order to be successful. You normally want to work from eight o'clock in the morning to five o'clock in the afternoon and then go for booze. If you are hard working you can get another job for two to four hours in the evenings or do something that generates more income. This extra income will help you realise your dream of buying a car or a house sooner. I have also seen in many African towns and villages young men who just sit idly around consuming alcohol or playing some kind of game or both. Most of these young men are married and they leave their wives and children at home. They expect their wives to do all the work in the fields and at the same time take care of the children. When they come home, they expect their wives to serve them food at the table. This is not right and it must change. Take an active role in the welfare of your family and the people around you. If you are unemployed, go to the fields and plant some crops. There is still plenty of unoccupied land in Africa. Let me tell you the story of my late stepbrother, Toto. Toto grew up a lazy boy who did not like going to school. He liked dancing very much and he would travel several kilometres every night to go dancing. This was alright as long as he was a teenager, but as he grew older, he had to begin taking care of himself. He could not get any employment because he was almost illiterate and did not learn any craftsmanship. Realising his situation, he decided to move to relatives who lived far away in a remote area. He was allotted five acres of very fertile land. He worked hard on this land and grew a lot of crops every year. This enabled him to live prosperously with his wife and children until his death.

As you grow older you will also be taking with you more responsibilities and a second job should never be out of question. If I could turn back the time, my motto would be "work first, enjoyment later". The early you can make more money the better it is for your future. In this context, I have another story of a very successful young German I met in Munich in the late nineteen seventies. I was working for a bank in Munich and every Friday, after work, I went out with some colleagues to a nearby pub to play billiards and have some drinks. After some months I got to know the owner of the pub very well. One day, in a casual conversation, he told me how hard he had to work to save money to set up a business. He told me that he lived in New York City for a few years and he had a normal job during the day, and in the evenings he used to wash dishes in Restaurants. When he returned to Germany he opened this pub. He was so successful within a short time that he opened up a chain of pubs in different parts of Munich. He was of course lucky because he happened to start the business at the right place and at the right time. The key is to be courageous and say as you go: "Yes, I can!"

CHAPTER FOUR

Marriage

According to the *Concise Oxford Dictionary*, marriage means "condition of man and woman legally united for purpose of living together and usually procreating lawful offspring". As you grow older, you will slowly begin to think of a partner on your side in your journey of life. In Africa there are many customs and traditions. I think some of these traditions and customs are out of date and it is time to adjust them to fit the modern times.

One such tradition is where the parents choose the partners and the bride and bridegroom get to see each other for the first time on their wedding day. Some of these marriages are happy ones, but most of them are usually unhappy. I think in the twenty first century every man and woman should be given a chance to choose his or her future partner. Remember that whoever you choose to be your partner is going to be close to you day and night for very many years. Don't rush into a marriage. Get to learn and know each other first, and before you decide to get married ask yourselves a simple question. Can she be a good mother to my children or can he be a good father to my children? Of course in Africa the purpose of marrying is to get children. If you have any doubt, don't marry, just stay as friends or break up. It might hurt to break up then, but it will even hurt more if you marry and the marriage breaks.

In Acholi, where I was born, customary marriage involves paying dowry. The amount of dowry is determined by the girl's parents. It can be in the form of money or cows or both. I think this custom is also out of date. I feel that if a certain man decides to marry my daughter, he is going to need some capital to start life with, together with my daughter. Moreover I do not want my daughter to feel that I am selling her off. I will be grateful to see them happy together. There is actually a discussion going on about this custom. Women feel that they are being sold off like property and sometimes subjecting them to harsh mistreatment. Although this custom has been there for many generations I would support its abolishment.

In certain societies in the world, women are still being treated as subordinates. They are denied the right to education and self determination. This is not fair and it is not right. Men in these societies must look forward and accept women as their equals. A custom or a tradition that was good during their grandparents' time is not necessarily good today in the twenty first century. In these societies, I have heard and read many times that in most cases a girl who refuses to marry a man chosen for her by her parents is killed to save the honour of the family. This is like living in the Stone Age. A girl must not be forced to marry anybody because it is her, and not her parents, who will spend the rest of her life with this man. The girl's interests are paramount and her decision should in no way bring dishonour to the family.

It was also customary for men in Africa to marry several wives and have many children. It was possible because they had plenty of cultivating land and big herds of cattle. Every woman had her own house and her cultivating land where she could plant anything she wanted. The women were all self sufficient because they could grow cotton for sale, millet, sesame, groundnuts, maize, cassava, potatoes and other vegetables for self consumption. My father was not an exception. He was married to four wives, including my mother, and we were twenty seven children altogether. This custom died a natural death, with a few exceptions, because it became unaffordable in the modern times. My advice to you young ones is—whatever your custom or tradition is, marry just one wife and keep an affordable family. It is easy to make children, but it is tough to raise them. For every child born, you must take the responsibility of feeding, clothing, and educating the child up to the University.

During my youth, and probably still up to today, it was a general belief that marrying and fathering children was a confirmation of manhood. This made young men marry early without any plans for the future. Some of them become fathers without any income. This forced the grandparents to come to their rescue. At a young age you do not foresee the repercussions of your actions. To get a sense, consider this: your parents have raised you up, educated you, and now they have to start all over again to take responsibility for the grandchildren. Is that fair? Some of you are so inconsiderate and continue to produce more children and dump them with the grandparents then go off to sleep again. Of course grandparents are always happy to take care of these children, but it should not be a permanent situation. The grandparents will even be happier to see how you affectionately raise up your own children, and they will always come in to help whenever their help is needed. My advice to you is—do not father a child until such a time that you can take full responsibility for it.

Children are the future. Without children this world will one day come to an end. Children look for love and leadership from you. They learn a lot from you as their parents and you should always love them. Never use violence in the presence of children. When children witness violence, they will themselves become violent because they think that it is the way to solve matters. A child that grows up in a family where domestic violence is widespread will himself be violent when he grows up. Domestic violence is rampant in African societies. This is probably because the men think that they are the absolute kings in the house and their actions or decisions are unquestionable. It is wrong. If you have a beloved wife, you should always consult her about a pending action or decision. In the end you make the decision anyway, but at least your wife is pleased that you consulted her. This brings harmony and avoids conflict which could end up in violence. It is natural for two people to have different opinions about something. You can discuss the matter and even if the opinions are so divergent, you should never use force to solve it. If a quarrel begins, sometimes it is good to leave the room or the area to allow tempers to cool down.

In any conflict between yourself and your wife, do your utmost best to keep your children out of it. The children did not choose to be born. You and your wife decided to make children and you enjoyed making them, so leave them out of any problems you may have. If your problems are so grave that you have to separate, try to come to some kind of understanding that does not hurt your children.

There is a custom, or may be a lifestyle, that is widespread in Africa which you must change. As I grew up, I saw that my brothers, relatives, and friends used to go out for drinks after work and returned home very late. When they got home, their wives used to get out of bed and serve them dinner. I thought it was quite a normal thing and when I got married I also demanded it from my wife. It was wrong.

One day, on one of my many visits to Uganda, I met a former school mate (Old Boy) in a local bar where I had gone for a drink. He told me he lived only a few metres away and he would be delighted if I could come to his home and meet his family and have dinner with them. I accepted the invitation because it was still very early in the evening. We continued to entertain ourselves and even more friends joined us. All of a sudden, it was midnight. I told him I would rather come and visit him the next day as it was already so late, but he insisted that I should accompany him and one of his friends joined us. When we arrived at his house, I looked at my Watch; it was nearly 01:00 a.m. His wife was already sleeping, but he woke her up. She got up, came and greeted us, and served us some drinks. Although she was very friendly, I did not feel comfortable about the situation. She started looking for firewood and making fire to prepare fresh millet bread and warm up the food she had prepared earlier. By the time we were finished with eating, it was already 03:00a.m. Please do not do this to your future wife. Put yourself in her situation. How would you feel? I would certainly not like it at all. As you continue with the journey of life, your slogan should be—**Treat others the way you would like them to treat you**.

Sometimes you have bad luck, your wife passes away. You will remarry, but before you remarry, make sure that the new wife will unequivocally accept your children as her own. I do not want to generalise, but lately, more and more cases of women mistreating their stepchildren are being reported. Some cases are so grave that you wonder whether these women have any heart at all. I have read many stories of stepmothers mistreating children and some are so gruesome that it can make you weep when you read it. The problem is that these stepmothers spend more time alone with these children, and when they mistreat or beat the children, they warn the children not to tell anybody about it otherwise they will get even worse treatment. Being afraid, the children know that they will be alone with her the next day so they keep quiet and continue to live unhappily with her. By the time their father finds out, it is probably too late because they are already too traumatised. Hence my advice to you guys is: before you marry another woman think of the wellbeing of your children.

The same advice applies to the hiring of domestic staff. These people spend the most time with your children, especially if both of you are employed. Most African families have domestic staff. These are normally relatives or acquaintances of relatives or of close friends. They are provided with accommodation and meals and paid a minimum wage. Unfortunately, these people work like slaves and nobody seems to care. They wake up early every morning, prepare the children for school, prepare and serve breakfast for all. As the children leave for school and the parents for work, they begin with house cleaning, washing dishes and clothes. Then they begin preparing lunch, which must be ready by the time the children and their parents come home. After lunch they have to clean the dishes and start with ironing. After ironing they start to prepare super. After super they help the children to wash themselves and then bring them to bed. By the time they are done for the day, it is nearly midnight. This is horrific. You will one day also employ domestic staff. Be fair to them. Offer them a decent wage and regulate their working hours. They are human beings like you and me and deserve the treatment you would like to be accorded to you.

You will by now have experienced that to get to know a girl intimately you first have to start flirting with her and then seducing her. Sex is a natural thing between a man and a woman and it should only happen through friendship and not by the use of force. Real men do not rape! Real men use the charm of seduction to bring girls to bed. If you were a girl, can you imagine how you would feel if you were raped?

How would you feel if your mother or your sister was raped? I personally would be very angry and disgusted. Rape is a crime and let us all deplore it. In some countries the woman raped is punished. She has either to marry the man who raped her or go to prison. This is not right and it is unacceptable. The man is stronger than the woman and if he uses force to invade a woman's privacy, he should be punished and not the woman. There are many girls out there and if you are a real man go out there and talk to them and with some charm you will win a heart. Unlike in my generation, today you have more opportunities through internet and the social networks to get to know a girl. Girls also like men—but only real men who can talk to them, crack jokes and laugh with them. Be a real man, don't rape!

CHAPTER FIVE

Politics

Politics is simply the art of influencing people. Political parties are organisations that seek to attain and maintain political power within government, usually by participating in electoral campaigns. Parties normally espouse expressed ideologies or visions bolstered by written platforms. This is not well understood by many people in Africa. Africans in power look at those in opposition as enemies and this is not right. It has happened many times that governments do not invite the opposition to the official independence anniversary celebrations. You should look at the opposition as friends who are also committed to solving the problems of the country but using policies different from those of the government. Each political party has a manifesto, an agenda and leaders.

In an election campaign, it is up to the party and its leaders to convince the masses that their manifesto and agenda is the best for the country at that given time. The party that can convince more people that its platform is the best wins and is entrusted with forming a government. If the elections were held on a level ground—transparent, and fair—the losing parties have to accept defeat and congratulate the winners. There should be no ground for huge euphoria or bitterness because voters have spoken and nation-building begins for all. Those who were elected will be judged in the next elections and those who lost will have their chance to prove that they are a better alternative.

Nation-building is not the duty of the government only; it is the duty of all citizens to participate in the shaping of the country's future and wellbeing. The winners should reach out to the losers so that they work together for the benefit of all people. The country does not belong to any political party or to any group of people. In a country with many ethnic or tribal groups, the composition of the government should reflect a balance of all these groups because no group should feel excluded from enjoying the fruits of independence.

All African countries have many tribal groups, and since independence, tribalism has caused many conflicts in many countries thereby impeding progress and development. The problem is with political leaders. When a leader of a political party comes to power, he tends to bring in his tribesmen to fill up most of the top government positions thus leaving the other tribes feeling alienated. Many leaders openly give development priorities to the areas they come from. Africa needs leaders who can stand above tribalism, leaders who have the interest of the country first, leaders who are committed to peace, justice, and democracy.

African leaders have failed to grasp the needs of the ordinary man, which is peace and security. At independence, the common man was happy to go to bed peacefully, wake up safely the next morning and go to work in his fields without fear of being killed by a mine. In many parts of Africa today, when you are going to bed, you do not know whether you will survive the night. If you survive the night, the next morning when you go digging in your field, you are worried that you may hit a mine and maim yourself. Dire poverty is so rampant that it has led to an immense increase in criminal activities day and night.

At independence, our leaders promised to fight to eradicate illiteracy, poverty, and disease. They promised to bring peace and prosperity to all. Today, five decades later, not a single African country has succeeded in eradicating even only one of these evils. Instead of bringing us prosperity they have brought us corruption. The leaders became too occupied with themselves. Their main concern was how they could stay in power for life. The result was military coup d'états and civil conflicts. Almost every African country went through some kind of conflict; Sudan had a very long civil war dating back to 1955 and ending with the split of the country into Sudan and South Sudan; Nigeria had the Biafra conflict in the nineteen sixties; Angola had a very long civil war which started in the nineteen seventies; Liberia had a civil war from 1989 to 2003; Sierra Leone had a civil war from 1991 to 2002; Rwanda had a genocide in 1994; Somalia is still in civil war since 1991. Till today, early 2013, there are insurgencies in Congo (Kinshasa), in Central African Republic, and in Mali. Most of these conflicts and insurgencies are caused by ethnic or tribal animosities.

Take Sudan for example, the north is mostly inhabited by Muslim Arabs and the south by Christian Africans. At independence in 1954, it was agreed among all parties that Sudan would become a federal republic with the north and south becoming semi-autonomies. However, after independence the central government in Khartoum, which was dominated by the northerners, did not grant part autonomy to the southerners, thus the beginning of the conflict. Sudan would probably be one big prosperous country today if hindsight and pragmatism had prevailed.

In a conflict or insurgency, no development takes place and all resources are wastefully diverted to the conflict. So a country like South Sudan has had no real peace and development for fifty years. Millions of children born in this time do not know what peace and prosperity is. Most of them were deprived of education and a chance to realise their dreams. The years of conflict were unproductive; many lives were lost and in the end nobody really gained, but all suffered.

So who is to blame here? I would put the blame on the political leaders, some of whom are deeply egoistic. They should talk to one another before the situation gets out of control. Most African presidents want their citizens to respect them as if they were God! Some of them believe they are the best and the only rulers ever born to rule a country. They can abolish or change the constitution according to their egos. They can use and spend government (taxpayer) money as they please.

One of these leaders, if I may mention, was the late Colonel Mohamed Gaddafi, who was the President of Libya. The Colonel did not know what democracy was, he did not know what institutions were; the Libyan treasury was his personal bank account. He engaged in dubious anti-Western activities. The money he wasted on these activities was enough to construct a superhighway from North Africa to South Africa and from West to East, which could have been named "Gaddafi Highway", after him. Another president worth mentioning here, but was not engaged in any dubious activities, was Joseph Mobutu. He was President of the Democratic Republic of Congo, which he later renamed Zaire. Democracy and Institutions were unknown words to him. Corruption was his speciality. It was reported that at the time of his overthrow, he had some five billion US dollars deposited in his personal accounts in Switzerland. Those presidents who overstayed in power benefited from the weak and divided opposition in those countries.

In countries with multiparty democracy, politicians want to form their own political parties. This leads to divisions and pleases the long-sitting president because the more the opposition is divided, the better are their chances of staying on and winning the elections. Sometimes I wonder whether the opposition parties are really serious about bringing change in their countries. The truth is—every politician has the ambition of one day becoming president, but in a field of five or more candidates, the incumbent has the best chance of being re-elected. The opposition would have a better chance if parties united and presented a united candidate.

It is equally important to win as many parliamentary seats as possible. This can only work if the opposition can agree on one candidate in each constituency. The party with the best chances of winning the constituency should be allowed to field the candidate for that constituency and all the opposition parties should actively support and campaign for this candidate. If the united opposition can capture more than forty percent of the parliamentary seats, it will make it difficult for the government to amend the constitution as it pleases, and even stop it from passing oppressive bills. Opposition politicians should refrain from attacking each other.

Uganda's President Museveni must have been grinning with a big, warm smile to read that the Democratic Party (DP) President, Mr. Norbert Mao, turned his guns on his archrival, Dr. Kizza Besigye. The DP President was reported to have described Dr. Besigye as a coward who was not fit to lead Uganda after President Yoweri Museveni left power, and warned DP supporters against backing him. First of all, Dr. Besigye has not announced nor has he indicated that he will be a candidate come 2016. I would personally characterize Mr. Mao's attack on Dr. Besigye as political madness. Instead of attacking the government for corruption and for its failures in delivering services to citizens, he is attacking a fellow opposition colleague who shares the same aspirations with him. I think people in

Uganda, like people in other African countries, genuinely want change, but they have nobody to turn to because the opposition is too divided. Quite honestly, the opposition parties in Uganda, Forum for Democratic Change, the Democratic Party, Uganda People's Congress, Uganda Federal Alliance, People's Development Party, and People's Progress Party, will never single-handedly take over power from the National Resistance Movement as long as Yoweri Museveni is president. It is unwise for each political party to field a presidential candidate against the incumbent. Voters want a clear alternative to the incumbent and also clear alternative Members of Parliament at the constituency level. If the opposition is to avoid the election debacle of 2011, where a candidate got 26.01%, and the other six candidates got a total of 5.6% of the votes, they have to form some kind of an alliance or a rainbow coalition and only nominate one candidate to run against the incumbent and also only one candidate in each constituency. This is the time to place the country above party politics. Voters will be given real alternative, one credible government candidate against one opposition candidate.

Some politicians may find it difficult to support a candidate from another party, but it is the only wise way to get to power. If Norbert Mao wants to contest again in 2016, he should be courting support from the other parties so that he is made the sole opposition candidate instead of attacking other opposition leaders. He is being divisive and reckless in attacking a fellow opposition comrade. The world is moving forward and so must Uganda and other African countries.

Let us forget the politics of the past that divided us and move forward in the spirit of unity and prosperity for all. For the sake of achieving change, political parties have to forget their differences and move forward in unity. It is like a football game where you have ten field players, some are tall and some are short, some are old and some are young, some are fast and some are slow; whatever characteristics they have, they have to play as a team in order to be successful.

Let me make one point very clear here. I am not interested in any political office and I have no ambition to stand for any elective office. At 65, I think I have lived my life and I am optimistically looking forward to the last day the sun sets on me. For the rest of my life and for the sake of my grandchildren, I will strive relentlessly to help leave this world a better, just and decent place to live in. I wish those leaders, who have ruled for more than a decade, could pause for a moment and look back at their achievements. They will realise that they have actually achieved most of the goals they set for getting to power. The longer they stay in power, the more repressive and dictatorial they become. There is absolutely no excuse for overstaying in power. Those who have overstayed in power and claim to be revolutionaries, who successfully fought bush wars, are just selfish, egoistic dictators. Africa should take great pride in Nelson Mandela. He did not personally wage a bush war, but he was at the forefront of the fight against apartheid and its institutions. For this just cause, he had to spend nearly three decades in prison. On his release, he was not vengeful, and only served one term as President of the Republic of South Africa. There was absolutely no doubt that he would have been overwhelmingly re-elected to a second term if he had chosen to run again.

Zimbabwe's Robert Mugabe is one of Africa's longest serving leaders. He was a successful bush war fighter. He inherited a very difficult situation when he came to power in 1980. At that time, seventy five percent of the most fertile land was owned by Zimbabwean whites who were less than five percent of the total population of Zimbabwe (see map on page 59). Prior to independence, there were negotiations in Lancaster House, in London, to agree on a common way forward to full independence. These talks led to the "Lancaster House Agreement". This agreement banned the Zimbabwean government from instituting land reforms for ten years. According to press reports at that time, the Africans attending the talks did not accept this, but after being assured of financial help to carry out the reforms, they agreed. After ten years, land reforms could be carried out on a "willing buyer, willing seller principle". Robert Mugabe's government honoured this agreement. When land reforms were eventually initiated, it was a very slow process and in order to speed it up, the Land Acquisition Act was enacted in 1992. The Act empowered the government to buy land compulsorily for redistribution, and a fair compensation was to be paid for every inch of land acquired. Landowners, who vehemently opposed the Act, could challenge the price set by the acquiring authority in court. I personally believe that President Robert Mugabe acted very responsibly here. He did not want to trigger an exodus of white Zimbabweans from the country. On the other hand, the majority African population expected him to deliver. No country in the world could tolerate 99% of the population cramming onto 25% percent of the country's land, leaving just 1% of the population in control of 75% of the country.

The British government also honoured its side of the agreement by providing financial help. However, in 1997, when the New Labour party came to power, the British government declared it did not accept that Britain had a special responsibility to meet the costs of land purchase in Zimbabwe. When the Lancaster House Agreement was signed in 1979, it must have been clear to all participants, including Britain, that any land reform would include purchasing of land from white Zimbabweans who owned 75% of Zimbabwean land. It was also clear then that in the long term the Zimbabwean government was not in a position to pay for all land purchases. If Britain, as a former colonial power, was interested in seeing a peaceful resolution of land issues in Zimbabwe, it could have appealed to the international community to come to the help of Zimbabwe. To me it looked as if Tony Blair's government was only interested in seeing Robert Mugabe's government fail, and consequently changed. I did not support all actions taken by Robert Mugabe, but I fully supported him on the issues of land. He waited for twelve years to start land reforms and promised full and fair compensation for all land compulsorily acquired.

It is unfortunate that the land reform exercise later became violent with some loss of life. The land issue was probably one of the reasons that forced him to cling to power for so long. My advice to him is to let the younger generation take over. He will be 90 years old in 2014, and it is time for him to take it easy and relax. He has served the country with dignity for over three decades for which many Zimbabweans are grateful. The best and most responsible and honourable thing for him to do is to retire now. The country is faced with great challenges in the 21st century, which require vigorous and dynamic leadership.

Even Pope Benedict XVI, who was younger than Mugabe, found it necessary to allow a younger and more vigorous person to take over leadership of the Catholic Church. There are many Zimbabweans capable of leading the country to prosperity. His treatment of the opposition in Zimbabwe was unfair and democratically unacceptable. For the sake of peace, the people of Zimbabwe should come together and ask President Robert Mugabe to retire and be left alone to live the rest of his life in peace. The opposition should also make it clear that they are not interested in reprisals or revenge for the injustices committed by the Mugabe government. Change is inevitable in Zimbabwe, and indeed many African countries. Politicians should be in a position to forgive and forget and move forward in the spirit of a fresh start. Reprisals and revenge attacks are wrong and should be avoided at all costs.

European area	
Tribal Trust land	
Native Purchase	
National land	

Labels on map: Kariba, Sinoia, Shamva, Salisbury, Wankie, Gatooma, Que Que, Umtali, Gwelon, Bulawayo, Fort Victoria, Shabani, West Nicholson, Triangle, Belt Bridge

Apportionment of land in Rhodesia (now Zimbabwe) in 1965

Some presidents run a one man show as if there is no Cabinet or ministers. Instead of staying above the day-to-day running of government as a statesman, they want to be everywhere and involved in everything. No president can run a country alone, which is why he appoints ministers to help run the country; and these are usually competent people who can work independently without constant public interference by him/her. Any minister the President deems incompetent can be dismissed at any time or in the next Cabinet reshuffle.

Power is very sweet, that is why in several African countries there are leaders who have overstayed in power. They are surrounded by "yes" men who encourage them to stay on. These people depend on him and will do whatever it takes to keep him in power. Some of these presidents have dozens of advisers who do not even meet him once in their entire tenure of office. Instead of improving the infrastructure, they create more districts in the name of bringing services closer to the people. The money spent in overhead expenses could be used to bring water (boreholes) to every village. People do not care about such services, which are not there anyway—they want water. In Africa, as you may see in the pictures in the next pages, women still walk several kilometres every day to fetch water. For women like these, creating a new district is of no importance at all. Having water close to them is of great help. They need water everyday for drinking, cooking, washing clothes, washing dishes, and bathing. That's the deal.

Governments should set priorities right. People need water, power, schools, and hospitals near them and these should be the top priority.

A woman returning home from fetching water with a baby tied on her back.

The same woman returning home from fetching water with a baby tied on her back. This was her fifth trip that day.

At a time when governments still depend on donor money, they should concentrate on development rather than on increasing administrative costs. Pictures like those above should be something of the past. There is so much waste in government. People complain of getting no medicine in hospitals and yet their presidents can afford to appoint more than forty state ministers, each with a government vehicle and a driver. Ministers have so called "wives" in all corners of the country, with luxury vehicles using government fuel. Utility vehicles, meant for government duties, are extensively used for personal purposes by ministers and top government officials.

If I were a minister, being driven around the country in a Mercedes Benz and I happen to pass by a school where lessons are being held under a tree, like in the pictures on the next pages, I would feel ashamed sitting in the luxury vehicle. Of course ministers and senior government officials need official cars, but do they have to be so luxurious and expensive? Look at the children learning under the tree; they are at the mercy of the weather. They stand a high risk of being killed by lightning. They cannot concentrate on their lessons due to distracting passers-by and other elements. They are continuously harassed by flies, mosquitoes, bees, and other insects—and sometimes snakes may pay a visit. Considering all these, it is disgusting to hear that some African presidents order and purchase armoured vehicles costing two million U.S. dollars a piece. Do these presidents have any morality at all?

A teacher conducts lessons under a tree in Uganda. (Source: Saturday Monitor). Classes being conducted under trees like here are not only found in Uganda but throughout Africa. **Isn't it shameful?**

Lessons being held under trees in Malawi. (Source: Malawi Teacher Professional Development Support).

It is true that African countries have development problems which cannot be solved within a short time. But if countries set right development priorities and get rid of corruption, Africa would take a big leap forward. Politicians should put the interest of the country first and focus all energy on development. Democracy, good governance, transparency, accountability and tolerance must become the cornerstone of decent politics in Africa. Besides, African governments should formulate legislation to regulate development as Africa moves forward and becomes more industrialised, but instead they are bringing laws restricting people's freedoms and suffocating the opposition.

Transparency in government is of paramount importance. Ruling without transparency erodes confidence and public trust in the government. A classical loss of trust and confidence in the government happened in Uganda. Since President Yoweri Museveni came to power in 1986, several prominent Ugandans died under suspicious circumstances. Every time a prominent person suspiciously died, the government promised a thorough investigation of the death. Indeed investigations were carried out and at one time the assistance of the British Scotland Yard was requested and given. That was great.

Unfortunately, the outcome of these investigations is never made public, and in most cases the families have never been informed. This raises suspicion among the public, who keep wondering whether the government had a hand in these killings. Such suspicion reached a climax in December 2012, when the Honourable Member of Parliament, Cerinah Nebanda, suddenly died. Cerinah was very young, just twenty four years old.

According to press reports, she was seen driving around Kampala city on the day of her death, which would imply she was healthy and in good spirits. When the news broke that evening that she was dead, an atmosphere of disbelief, consternation, anger and suspicion developed. Many people were deeply touched by her death. Since her death was not caused by an accident, people widely suspected that such an abrupt death could only have been caused by poisoning. The main suspect was the government. Many people suspected, and many more even believed, that the government had a hand in her abrupt death. This was because of the lack of transparency the opaque government had demonstrated in investigation of past deaths. People just assumed that the government had a hand in these deaths, which was why it did not want to make the findings public.

Now listen to this. The President paid a visit to the deceased's mother to personally convey his condolences and that of the government and the people of Uganda. During this honourable visit, he emphasised that the government did not have a hand in the young Parliamentarian's death and promised a thorough and quick investigation into her death. There was absolutely no reason not to believe him. I personally believed he was telling the truth. He liked Cerinah (RIP) and would not even have thought of doing anything that would have harmed her. He was understandably hurt when people widely suspected him and his government to have had a hand in her death. This anger resulted in his outburst at a press conference, where he called those who alleged that his government was involved in her death "idiots and fools". I personally think he went too far here. It does not matter how angry he was, nothing justified him calling his subjects idiots and fools. These are the people who made him President through their vote. Were they idiots and fools to have voted for him? He would have avoided this anger in the first place if his government had exhibited transparency by publishing the findings of earlier investigations.

Due to lack of transparency and the pain of the death of this young member, Parliament resolved to carry out its own investigation. This was because each time the executive branch of government undertook to investigate a suspicious death, the legislative branch was never given the findings. The Speaker of Parliament, who was in deep shock, asked three MPs, members of the ruling party who were also medical doctors, to go to the hospital and attend the post-mortem examination. That examination later confirmed that a heavy substance crushed Cerinah's pancreas and lungs, which is what caused her death. Further toxicological analysis was deemed necessary. According to press reports, it was decided, in the presence of the Police Commissioner, to take a sample and divide it into two—one for the government, the other for Parliament (and the deceased's family). Since no laboratory in Uganda had needed facilities to do this toxicological analysis, Parliament requested a government pathologist to take the sample to a laboratory in South Africa.

This became a golden opportunity for the President and his government to prove to the country and the world that he and his government were not involved in killing innocent citizens and had had no hand in the death of the honourable Member of Parliament. But again the government missed this golden opportunity, because it did not allow Parliament to take the sample to South Africa for analysis. If the sample had been independently analysed, the result would have probably exonerated the government. It would thus not automatically be under suspicion in any future strange deaths. If, by law, only the police had been allowed to carry out this sort of investigation, the government should have made an exception and allowed the pathologist to fly to South Africa under a police escort, but this wasn't done. Makes one wonder who advised these men of power.

Events that followed can only be labelled blunders. The pathologist was arrested at the airport and later suspended; and the sample was confiscated and later flown to a laboratory in London. The government (the police) should have realised that they were not dealing with a group of thugs, but with legislators who enacted the laws of the country. If Parliament felt that an independent investigation into the matter was necessary, they should have been allowed to do so without hindrance or the threat of arrest. Maybe members should pass a law today allowing them to independently investigate matters of importance to them, or pass a law forcing the executive to always give a copy of the findings of investigations to the Speaker of Parliament.

On the other hand, Members of Parliament should also not engage in insinuations or utterances that have no substance. Through the press, I was made to understand that due to this matter, some Members of Parliament spent a night in their offices in Parliament for fear of being arrested if they left the building. This would not have been necessary if the Ugandan Parliament had enacted laws guaranteeing their immunity from arbitrary arrest.

I want to recommend that all African Parliaments amend the constitution to give Parliamentarians immunity from arrest. Many European countries have this constitutional protection since the nineteenth century. This is to protect members of the legislative branch from arbitrary arrests and trumped up charges by the executive branch of the government.

In some countries, you can impeach and remove a president from office, but you will require a two thirds majority of votes in Parliament. This would not be possible in a country like Uganda today because Members of Parliament are not protected from arbitrary arrests. If an impeachment process was started, the President could theoretically direct the arrest of half of the members on trumped up charges before the vote so that Parliament could never get the required two thirds majority. Immunity from arrest does not protect a member who engages in criminal activities. Once the Police have evidence that one has committed a crime, they can apply to the Speaker to have the immunity lifted. The Speaker then convenes a meeting of the committee on immunities within forty eight hours, and if the evidence against the member is convincing, the immunity is lifted and the police and the member in question are informed accordingly.

Although we live in an era of independence, some African governments still find it convenient to use colonial laws to harass citizens. In August 2012, South African miners in an industrial dispute were slaughtered like animals as you can see in pictures on the next pages. Footage of the cold blooded shooting can be seen in *YouTube*. No single life should be lost in an industrial dispute or in a peaceful demonstration. The police should have used all means at their disposal, even using water cannons and tear gas if need be, before firing a single shot. Besides, politicians should have stepped in before the conflict became violent. It is easy to set up a judicial commission of inquiry afterwards, but this does not bring life back to the dead.

The most bizarre thing here was that over two hundred miners were arrested and initially charged with murder, under a little-known "common purpose" legislation previously used by the apartheid government. The world watched how the police fired shots and killed the miners, and at the end these same miners were charged with the murder of their colleagues. Unbelievable! This was indeed a crime against humanity. Initially no police officer was charged. The minister in charge of the police should have taken responsibility and resigned. The ANC government should be ashamed of the shootings and should urgently repeal all such unfair apartheid laws.

South Africa's Lonmin Marikana mine clashes killed 34 miners. (Source: BBC News)

Policemen inspect after firing shots at protesting miners outside a South African mine in Rustenburg, 100 km. northwest of Johannesburg, August 16, 2012. (Source: National Post, Canada).

Protesting miners react as the police shot at them, August 16, 2012. (Source: National Post, Canada)

A policeman collects weapons that were supposedly used by protesting miners, August 16, 2012. (Source: National Post, Canada).

Is the ANC government really in charge of power in South Africa? Events happening there give a negative impression. First of all, the massacre of the Marikana mine workers should never have happened. The government should have intervened early enough. The mineworkers were justifiably asking for a wage increase and the mine companies should have gone a longer distance to meet their demands. Over several decades, the mine companies have been making millions of profits every year on the back of the miners. This cannot go on forever. It is the duty of the companies to explain to the shareholders that they have to be prepared for lesser dividends in order to accommodate workers demands.

If the companies had refused to yield to the workers' demands, the government should have stepped in and tried to find a middle-way out. It would have been much better if the government had appointed a commission to negotiate a settlement between the parties rather than appoint a commission to investigate the massacre. Secondly, the miners should have never been charged with the murder of their colleagues under an apartheid-era "common purpose" doctrine; this was embarrassing and somebody in the government should have taken political responsibility and resigned. According to the South African constitution, the Justice Minister "must exercise final responsibility over the prosecuting authority". The minister failed and brought shame and disrepute on the ANC government.

Another event that appears to make the ANC government powerless in South Africa happened at the end of April

2013. A privately chartered plane, Airbus A330, was given permission to land at the Waterkloof Air Force Base. The plane was reported to be carrying about 200 guests from India, who were invited to a family wedding. The passengers allegedly bypassed customs procedures on their way to a gaudy entertainment complex. It is further alleged that the wedding guests were transferred from the military base to Sun City by a private security company in black BMWs equipped with illegal emergency lights and false registrations.

This was incredible. How could such things have happened in a country and the government did not have a clue? Is there a secret, parallel authority in South Africa that is equally as powerful as the ANC government? This is very disturbing. Here again the ANC government promised to investigate, but did it? This government, under President Jacob Zuma, has now been in power for nearly 5 years and should by now be well acquainted with governing. In many instances it has been ruling by reacting rather than acting. Good governing requires action before a matter or a situation gets bad or out of control. Zuma was elected to govern and not to sit by and wait for things to take their course and then react. Commissions of inquiry only help to rectify wrongs done due to inaction!

Twenty years after apartheid, the ANC government is in a strong position to offer Lesotho annexation talks. During the years of apartheid rule in South Africa, it was understandable that Lesotho chose to remain an independent sovereign state. Looking at the map of South

Africa today, one wonders how an independent state can exist in the middle of it and completely surrounded by it (see map next page). Lesotho should become part of South Africa as the tenth province and annexation is the best logical solution for the people living there. Those in favour of annexation in Lesotho should force the government to hold a binding referendum on annexation. It is likely that more than two thirds of the population will be in favour of it. Annexation will be beneficial to both countries. Opposition will most likely come from those who stand to lose their power, like the Prime Minister, ministers, and other high-ranking government officials. It is in the nature of all human beings that once you have power to exercise over people, you would not want to voluntarily give it up. However, in this case, for the people of Lesotho, the benefit of annexation is great indeed and should be pursued.

Lesotho: right in the middle of South Africa.

Back in Uganda, an old, sickening colonial law which allowed "preventive house arrest" is frequently used by the government to harass citizens. The law is being used to restrict the movements of certain individuals (mostly the opposition) for as long as the government wants. This law was used by the colonialists before independence to curtail the movement of the nationalists who were fighting for self rule and independence. Today a free and fully independent country should not find it necessary to revert to colonial style rule, because it speaks of fear and insensitivity.

All over Africa, in big towns or cities, there is the problem of slums. A slum is a neighbourhood with minimal or no basic services such as sanitation, with no investment that keeps costs so low that the poorest of the poor can afford them. These slums have been there since independence and they have grown bigger and bigger. We can afford to build skyscraper after skyscraper yet these people in the slums do not even have a toilet to ease themselves. Think of the many children being born there every day—what chances have they got in life? Let us not leave these people behind as we move on with development. If a country is serious about helping these people, it can draw up an upgrade plan and ask donors for financial help. Even wealthy individuals and Non Governmental Organisations may probably chip in. I was informed that Sweden donated five million dollars in 2005 for Kibera, in Nairobi, and this was probably why upgrade work started and took root there.

It has been reported recently, April 2013, that in the slums of Kampala, we have children who go to bed hungry. I was shocked and ashamed to hear a young girl tell a reporter that she would sometimes go two days without eating any food. When she was told that a chess club nearby offered its members a cup of porridge everyday, she joined it so that she could at least drink some porridge instead of going to bed hungry. She was not the only child going to bed hungry daily; there are thousands of children out there starving everyday. Those living in slums are not there by choice, but by circumstances. It is the task of African governments to make sure that every child, every woman, and every man gets a just and decent living. This is not a privilege, but a birthright. Every child, every woman, and every man is entitled to equal educational, job, and health opportunities irrespective of his/her ethnic or tribal origin. We in Africa cannot be proud of ourselves without solving the slum problem. See slum pictures in the next pages.

Kisenyi Slum in Kampala. (Source: AcTogether.blogspot.)

Nairobi, Kibera slum (Source: media disciplesupport.)

A slum in Addis Ababa (Source: Power of peace).

CHAPTER SIX

Institutions

An institution is an organisation, an establishment, a foundation, a society or the like, devoted to the singular promotion of particular causes or particular programs. Its characteristics are: continuity, stability, predictability, and security. When you start talking about institutions, you can begin from marriage and other civil entity, to religion, to state, and finally to government. A state is an organised political community, living under a government. A government is the system by which a state or a community is governed. We are into definitions now, aren't we?

A government consists of legislators, administrators, and arbitrators. Government is the means by which state policy is enforced, as well as the mechanism for determining the policy of the state. A form of government, or form of state governance, is the set of political systems and institutions that make up the organisation of a specific government. States are served by a continuous succession of different governments. Each successive government is composed of a body of individuals who have control over political decision-making. Their function is to make and enforce laws and arbitrate conflicts. In Africa today, 2013, there are five types of government namely; a) Democracy; b) Autocracy, c) Despotism, d) Dictatorship, e) Kleptocracy.

a) Democracy is the rule by a government chosen by election where most of the populace are enfranchised. The right to vote is not limited by a person's wealth or race. The main qualification for enfranchisement is usually having reached a certain age. A Democratic government is therefore one supported by a majority of the populace, provided the election was held fairly.

b) Autocracy is rule by one individual whose decisions are subject to neither external restraints nor regularized mechanisms of popular control.

c) Despotism is rule by a single entity with absolute power. That entity may be an individual or it may be a group.

d) Dictatorship is rule by an individual who has full power over the country. This may refer to a system where the dictator came to power and holds it purely by force; but it also includes systems where the dictator first came to power legitimately but then was able to amend the constitution so as to, in effect, gather all power for himself. Usually, there is little or no attention to public opinion or individual rights.

e) Kleptocracy is a rule by thieves; a system of governance where officials and the ruling class pursue personal wealth and political power at the expense of the wider population. (In strict terms, kleptocracy is not a form of government, but a characteristic of a government engaged in such behaviour).

I leave it to you to decide on the system of governance in your country, but for sure few fall under category (a). On the other hand, all Western countries fall under this category. They have strong, independent, and respectful institutions. Human rights are largely respected and everybody is treated equally before the law. Let me give you two examples of strong institutions in Germany.

One Saturday evening, in the city of Hanover, the police noticed a VW Phaeton car driving past a red traffic light. They stopped the vehicle, which was driven by a lady in her early fifties. As they were checking her identity, they smelled some alcohol inside the vehicle. They politely asked her if she'd drank any alcohol that evening. She answered in the affirmative, but quickly added that it was only one glass of wine, nothing more.

The law in Germany, at that time, allowed one to drink and drive with a maximum of 0.5 "Promille", which is the equivalent of one small glass of wine, and this too depended on one's body size. Since the lady confessed having drunk some alcohol and she drove through red traffic light, the police decided to take her to the station for blood test. The test confirmed that she must have drunk more than what she confessed to have drunk. It showed that she had more than double the value of alcohol in her blood than the allowed amount for driving. She had to surrender her driving permit there and then. This lady was a very important person (VIP) and it was known to the police all along. She was the chairman/woman of the Evangelical

Church in Germany, the equivalent of the Anglican Archbishop in Germany. She resigned from her position in order not to damage the honour of the institution. She was accorded the same treatment you and me would have gotten. Wasn't that great? This definitely would not have happened in any African country.

The second example happened in 2012, and the matter is still in court. An affair, which started in November 2011, led to the resignation of the tenth President of the Federal Republic of Germany, Christian Wulff. He was accused of accepting bribes (corruption) during his time as Minister-President (Prime Minister) in the state of Lower Saxony (Niedersachsen). It was alleged that two of his holidays were financed by his business friends. He accepted that it may be true, but he refunded them the money they paid and denied any wrongdoing right from the start. When the Director of Public Prosecutions (DPP) in Hanover successfully requested that his immunity be lifted, he resigned to avoid putting the institution of President into contempt. At the beginning of April 2013, the DPP offered to drop the case if he agreed to pay a fine of twenty thousand Euros. He refused the offer because he believed he was innocent. The courts will decide the case.

There are two points to note here. First of all, due to the strong institutions in this country, the DPP was able to take on and force the resignation of the man holding the highest office in the land. Secondly, the office bearer demonstrated a great character and a high political maturity by resigning immediately, leaving the institution unscathed. Africa should take lessons from these examples. Strong institutions are essential for just and democratic rule.

Western countries have remained democratic because of the laws and regulations guiding institutions. From the President or Prime Minister to the ministers, legislators, judges, and civil servants, there are rules and regulations they follow in performing their duties. This is what African countries badly need. It cannot be right that an African president can spend the tax payers' money at will. Why are budgets passed by Parliament if the head of government does not care about it? In 2011, in Uganda, the President was reported to have spent US$ 740 million on Russian military jets. Apparently this money was not budgeted for and it was spent at a time teachers had asked for salary increase and they were told that there was no money.

In a poor country like Uganda, it is unfortunate that so much money is wasted on metal junk. I call them metal junk because after some years use they will become junk. Moreover, fuel and maintenance costs spiral into more millions every year. I was amused and at the same time amazed when I turned my TV on and saw President Museveni donating a sack of money to Busoga Youth Forum (see pictures next page). I have nothing against donating money this way, but I think it would have been better if the youth organisation had registered with the President's office, outlining needs and the President disbursed the money by cheque as funds became available.

This way the President would have kept a record of the pledges fulfilled and when. Uganda's institutions are weak, that is why there is massive corruption in the country. Everything in the country has to go through the President. He laments about the corruption in a country he rules, yet he should realise that it is him who opens the door for corruption through his actions. He cannot keep details of actions he authorised, and government officials know this and they take advantage of it. In 2011, the President ordered the compensation of a businessman for the loss of an agreed-upon deal on Kampala markets. The businessman was paid about 150 billion shillings (over US$ 55 million). When the President got to know about the amount paid, he was surprised and complained about the excessive amount. The President should realise that his involvement in certain matters, like this one, always opens the door to corruption. Two Cabinet ministers resigned over this affair, but the damage had already been done.

President Museveni at the handover of a sack containing two hundred fifty million shillings (US$ 100.000,-). (Source: Daily Monitor)

Busoga Youth chairperson carrying the sack of currency notes donated by President Museveni on his head. (Source: Daily Monitor).

Why should the President have been involved here? There were courts of law in the country and government authorities who could have handled this matter. In April 2013, the *Daily Monitor* carried a headline, "Museveni gives out more Kitante land". The story was that he had given an investor in 2007, 10.7 acres of land in Kitante for a hospital project. The project was to start then and the first phase was supposed to have been completed in 2012. The *Daily Monitor* reported that there has been no construction work at the site given to the investor six years ago, apart from a brick-making business on the compound.

The *Daily Monitor* further reports that the investor has gone back to the President requesting more land. If the request is granted, the piece of land will probably be carved out of Kitante School land (see picture next page). My concern here is this—why did the investor go directly to the President in the first place? There are institutions in place, like the Uganda Land Commission, and the Kampala City Council Authority. Are these institutions incapable of handling such matters? If you want to invest in London do you go to the British Prime Minister? No. No. No. This is not the norm for doing business. If Africa is to move forward, we should give institutions a chance and not allow corruption to creep in.

Kitante Primary School pupils stand near the fence that separates the school from the five acres given to the investor to build a hospital. (Source: Daily Monitor).

CHAPTER SEVEN

Corruption

Corruption is moral impurity or deviation from an ideal. Corruption may include many activities including bribery and embezzlement. Government corruption occurs when an office holder or employee acts in an official capacity for his or her own personal gain. Corruption can occur on many different scales. There is corruption that occurs as small favours between a small number of people. There is corruption that affects the government on a large scale, and corruption that is so prevalent that it is part of the every day structure of society. Factors which encourage corruption include conflicting incentives, discretionary powers, monopolistic powers, lack of transparency, low pay, and a culture of impunity. Specific acts of corruption include bribery, extortion, and embezzlement in a system where corruption becomes the rule rather than the exception. Corruption can occur in many different economic sectors, whether it is public or private industry or even NGOs.

Africa is the most corrupt continent in the world and this has hampered development. Corruption is a vice comparable to an infectious disease. It is infested in governments and all walks of life. The fight against corruption is a very difficult one because of the temptations involved. Many countries today are trying hard to stop it. I was very much impressed by the achievements of the Nigerian Economic and Financial Crimes Commission, under the chairmanship of

Mr. Nuhu Ribado. It was reported that he brought more than one thousand cases to court, and of these he secured two hundred convictions. He even managed to send his own boss, the Inspector General of Police, to prison. He was offered a cash bribe of US$ 15.000.000. He took the cash and deposited it with the Central Bank and later used it as an exhibit in the trial against the briber. He was forced to leave the country because several attempts were made on his life. He deserves respect and admiration for his steadfastness. Many cases of corruption were reported in Nigeria in the last three decades. In 2009, United States investigators traced US$ 150,000,000 in bribes on Swiss bank accounts given to Nigerian Officials. This was part of a bribe of a total amount of US$ 180,000,000 paid to Nigerian officials between 1994 and 2004 to secure contracts worth 6 billion dollars. The good news here is the US government punished the executives involved in paying these bribes to prison terms and money fines. Several companies were also fined a total of over a billion dollars.

African countries should also pass laws that punish those who offer bribes just as those who take the bribes. Maybe this could discourage companies from offering bribes in order to win contracts. Company executives should also be held personally responsible for all shoddy work done in the performance of a government tender and/or contract. In some countries, corruption is so deeply embedded that it will take several generations to uproot it. In my country, corruption has reached supernatural levels and we now call it "Ghost Corruption". It starts at a junior level and ends at a very senior level. Since the introduction of Universal Primary Education Scheme, schools have been reporting an inflated number of pupils (ghost pupils) in their schools. Under this scheme, the government pays for the pupils' education and the more pupils each school reports, the more money the government pays to the school. Then there are ghost teachers, ghost soldiers, and ghost civil servants. All these employees get paid by the government, including the ghosts. There were also ghost pensioners who alone, over some years, cost the government 300 billion shillings (about 120 million US dollars). Another loss incurred by the government worth mentioning here was the payment of 1.7 million US dollars for the purchase of bicycles for local council chairmen in 2011. The money was paid to a non existent company and was never recovered.

Why do we Africans tend to be so corrupt? I think the answer lies in our lifestyle. We tend to live beyond our means at any given time. If I earn 500 dollars a month, I cannot afford to live a lifestyle that costs me 1.000 dollars a month, yet this is the way we live. Many government officials have large families to support. Some of them have one or two girlfriends whom they also support. On top of that they want to go out drinking every night. The money they earn is not enough to maintain this lifestyle. This leads to corruption by accepting bribes. If we are to succeed in fighting corruption, we have to start to live within our financial means. That's it!

CHAPTER EIGHT

Energy and Environment

There is an acute shortage of electricity in almost all African countries. It is not unusual to have blackouts in towns and cities in many countries. Power infrastructure is also poor in almost all African countries. It is unfortunate that Africa has not been making effective use of renewable energy, like solar power and wind power. The sun shines everyday throughout the year in most parts of Africa. Africa should have been leading research in solar and wind energy and today there would be no blackouts. It is not too late to begin to invest in these sources of renewable energy. Governments should make solar panels affordable to citizens by reducing or eliminating taxes on these products. All new buildings should be fitted with solar panels. The energy won from the solar panels is enough to cater for all day household needs, like air conditioning, refrigerating, water heating and cooking. This would, on the other hand, help to alleviate pressure on industrial power usage during the day.

Governments could also consider establishing power plants in small towns, using wind turbines and or solar panels. These are sources of very clean renewable energy. African countries would be well off following Germany's example, which is now undergoing energy revolution.

Germans should be grateful to the Green Party, which has consistently opposed nuclear power since its formation in 1980. The Greens have been winning votes campaigning on ecological and anti nuclear platforms. Pro-nuclear power companies have always insisted that nuclear power was clean, cheap, and safe, but the Fukusima nuclear disaster proved them wrong. This nuclear disaster forced the German government of Christian Democrats and Free Democrats to reverse their pro-nuclear policies. All nuclear power stations will be shut down by the end of 2022. Germany has now embarked on a revolutionary system of energy production through renewable sources. These renewable sources include water turbines, wind turbines, and solar panels. African countries should keep a close watch at Germany's progress.

———

I have said what's been burning in my heart. I'm aware that most African leaders will turn a blind eye to my recommendations and instead seek ways to ban this book or do me harm. I wish they opened their eyes. Regardless of their paranoia, I make a covenant with the African youth today—that if my recommendations are adopted by future generations, Africa will emerge stronger and will become a global leader in democracy, business and other areas of human interest. Let's go forward without fear because the future belongs to the brave!